Simple Tools for Stillness

Following the Way of Jesus

Wanda Nash

Author and Christian Speaker

GROVE BOOKS LIMITED
RIDLEY HALL RD CAMBRIDGE CB3 9HU

Contents

Dedication

Be an honour to thy church, follow Christ's word
clear in thy task and careful in thy speech;
be thine an open hand, a merry heart,
Christ in thy mouth.
Live that all may know a lover of righteousness and compassion;
let none come to thee and go sad away.

St Alcuin 735–804 AD

Note

In this publication, simply for convenience and brevity, the Godhead will be referred to as 'he/his/him.' No gender is implied. Several versions of the Bible have been used in the preparation of this book with the following abbreviations: The Authorized Version King James Bible (1611), AV; Christian Community Bible (2002), CCB; Revised English Bible (1989), REB; New Jerusalem Bible (1990), NJB; New Standard Revised Version (1991), NRSV.

The Cover Illustration is by Peter Ashton

First Impression February 2005
ISSN 0262-799X
ISBN 1 85174 586 6

Introduction 1

'Stillness' is the word used in Scripture.

We complicate it by using long words like contemplation, meditation, relaxation, imagination, visualization. Jesus said simply, 'Come to me and rest.' This book is simple; it is about being still with God.

Why on earth should we want to be still? There are so many demands and needs, causes and concerns to attend to, so many enticements and excitements to arouse us—the last thing I want to be is still! Rest is for those who are weary, weak or worried; surely it is only for those who are not coping well? In this book we may find that God, the source of all wisdom, planned things differently.

'Tools' is another simple word. The Oxford Dictionary describes 'tools' as 'things needed in pursuit' of a certain occupation, like the crook of a shepherd, the lathe of a carpenter, the ears with which we hear—all provided by God. If our pursuit is a closer watch with God, we should be aware of the tools he himself has provided so we can fit in with his view of the world. In the next chapters these tools are both described and used.

Fr Gregory, the founder of the Order of Julian, put it like this:

> The basic human stance before God is to *await, allow, accept, attend.* Identifying our true selves with silent listening has been a problem in today's world. If the church is to survive the storm of our age, it will be by the rediscovery of this fundamental stance before God. This is the stance from which wise teaching, true leadership and gifted authority will naturally and even beautifully flow.[1]

I was hooked into stillness as far back as I can remember. Every three years or so of my childhood I was sent, not just for a while but permanently, to another continent—not another house or school or country, but another continent. This frequent dislocation from everything I knew led me to rely more and more on the stability of the deep still place within, a place of deepest privacy, often unguessed at by others, a place that is unique and difficult to communicate in words. God knows it through and through, for God himself places it there, in each one of us. This depth within us needs to be established, strengthened and celebrated in God's company, for it is there that the God-made-me comes in contact with the God-who-made-me, and where the self-made-me can gradually fade.

This is the hidden place from which we gift each other, from which we welcome one another as guests, teachers, and partners, instead of being burdens, snares and distractions, a place where we can access and offer what Rowan Williams frequently calls *self-gift*. To find that deep root we need to be still and silent, aware and attentive before God—without jabbering our anxieties or plying our demands, simply there for him to mould.

And this is the strange paradox: in no way am I worthy to touch the hem of his garment, and yet Dame Julian writes that I am 'garmented' by God. I am be-clothed by God, enclosed within him.[2] Receiving from God whatever it is that he wants me to receive, with the barriers of my own suppositions, projections and ambitions well out of the way. There we receive moments of deep touching and anointing. There the present moment, his presence, and the presents he longs to give us all meld together.

Stories often help. This is one I like:

> There were three brothers who lived with their father. After he had died, they wondered about their future. The eldest brother said, 'I'm off to give health to the world.' The second brother said: 'I'm off to spread education around the world.' And the third brother said 'I'm staying here.'
>
> A year or two passed and the eldest brother returned. He said 'I am exhausted and dis-eased.' The second brother came home and said 'I am weary and confused.' The third brother said, 'Wait here: I'm going to fetch some water from the river.'
>
> He came back with a bowl full of water. It was thick and murky, but he asked his brothers to sit round it and silently watch it. Gradually the water settled, and the mud fell to the bottom; the water became so clear the brothers could see their faces reflected in it. The peace of the stillness enveloped them.
>
> 'You see,' said the youngest, 'it is only when you are still enough to know your own faces, that you can hear what God wants of you. Only then can you act in God's power.'

Always, as we explore the tools which help us to get there, we shall be following the ways of Jesus Christ as he modelled them for us in the gospels. Perhaps the strangest thing of all is this: Jesus, the Son of God, was provided by his Father with the same tools as we are. He just used them a lot better.

Why 'Stillness'?   2

What a strange thing to do.

To waste time—consciously; to let go of energy—deliberately; to become emptied and vulnerable—on purpose. Probably time, energy and autonomy are among our most treasured attributes; it seems crazy to choose to drop them, even temporarily. But where we find deep desire to clear the stage, to get away from all the structures and status and scaffolding that support us, that is the way to do it. Sometimes it means a steely desire to put aside the crutches, justifications and displays that hold us upright daily, so that space can be made for God, for God to be God as God is, and not as we make God out to be.

Thomas Traherne, in the 16th century, was wise. He said that in order to fill a bucket you first have to empty it—not just add to what it already holds, but turn it upside down and empty it. And then I must allow the Holy Spirit to refill it, in his way, not mine.

Jesus and His Priorities

Jesus' priorities for every day of his ministry were immense and astonishing. His job description became clear to him: crowds to teach; multitudes to heal; thousands to love. His clear task was to bring in the kingdom of God. With all these pressures and expectations and demands to bear, we read that he consciously, deliberately, and on purpose chose to withdraw for a time, in order to disengage, disentangle and disencumber himself, before his Father.

In the gospels, Jesus' inclination to 'go into that secret place' where he would meet his Father privately is mentioned over 40 times.[3] Few people had their 'own room' in the Palestine of that era. Each house was made up of rooms looking out on to a communal courtyard, and one room would be occupied by a whole family. The 'secret room' (Matt 6.6) talked of by Jesus is the hidden place inside oneself, where prayer is 'with your Father who is with you in secret.' Jesus himself modelled it for us. He would leave important meetings, times of strong personal affirmation, and even the heat of conflict. His foremost priority, in spite of the workload he was called to do and the minimal time he had to do it, was to listen to God in that secret, deep, stillness.

To Nicodemus, to the woman at the well in Samaria, and in answer to the questioning Greek visitors, Jesus stressed that prayer is 'of the Spirit'; it is of the breath and the wind, no-one knows from where it comes or to where it is going. It is about making contact with the Godhead, driven by the Spirit, from a depth we cannot fully comprehend. It is about creating room in my head, my heart, and my hands to wait for 'the still small voice' that God uses 'in that secret place.'

Among those stories in 2 Kings that prefigure the ministry of Christ is a wonderful analogy of this prayer beyond words. A woman comes to Elisha in great distress because the creditors are after her, following the death of her husband. 'I have nothing,' she cries out, 'nothing except a small pot of oil.' Elisha tells her to go into her house with as many empty pots as she can gather, and lock the door. There, unseen by others, something happens. All the pots get filled, all from her own small pot. Not only is there enough oil to repay her creditors, but the empty pots belonging to her neighbours get filled too (2 Kings 4.1–7). It is an apt metaphor for what happens in that still room. The empty vessel gets refilled, but in so doing the other emptinesses are attended to as well.

The Pattern in the Old Testament

Jesus' references to prayer are rooted in his profound knowledge of the Scriptures. For instance, in Isaiah we read, 'Go, my people, enter your rooms, and shut the doors after you; withdraw for a little while' (Isa 26.20). In our modern rushed lives it is startling that over and over again in the Old Testament God continually speaks of rest. It is offered to his people as a command ('In returning and rest shall you be saved,' Isa 30.15), as a resource ('This is the rest wherewith you may cause the weary to rest, this is the refreshing,' Isa 28.12) and as a reward ('Ask for the old paths, where is the good way, and you shall find rest for your souls,' Jer 6.16).

As so often happens today, each offer is refused. We read the people's reaction—'and you would not'…'Yet they would not hear'…and 'But they said, we will not walk therein.' Eventually the psalmist puts God's response in these words: 'Forty years long was I grieved with this generation and said, this is a people that do err in their hearts…they shall not enter into my rest' (Ps 95.10–11). It is as if the rest offered by God was his ultimate gift, and to withhold it is his ultimate sanction.

Silence, stillness and rest are words scattered throughout the Old Testament. The Sabbath itself was a day of rest, and distinguished the Jews from the pagan religions around them. Even Solomon was told: 'Behold, a son shall be born to you, who shall be a man of rest; and I will give him rest from all his enemies (1 Chron 22.9). Others include: 'Issachar saw that rest was good' (Gen 24.15); 'My presence shall go with thee and I will give you rest' (Ex 33.14); 'The spirit of the Lord shall rest upon him…and his rest shall be glorious' (Isa 11.2, 10); and 'Rest in the Lord,' where the Hebrew literally means 'Be silent to the Lord' (Ps 37.7).

'Silence' and 'stillness' carry frequent messages. Some of the most relevant are: 'Their strength is to sit still' (Isa 30.7); 'Only be silent, and let silence be your wisdom.' (Job 13.5 REB); 'Be silent, and I shall teach you wisdom' (Job 33.33 REB); 'Return to thy stillness, O my soul, for the Lord has dealt bountifully with thee' (Ps 116.7). So it was from this foundational knowledge that Jesus himself said, 'Set your troubled minds at rest; trust in God always' (John 14.1).

The Transition

Perhaps there were other influences behind Jesus' practice of constant withdrawal. From around 500 years before Jesus' lifetime, Jewish leaders themselves were building up a tradition of approaching God in stillness. The tenets were passed from teacher to searcher by word of mouth because the subject was considered too precious to be squandered amongst ordinary worshippers, and therefore it was hidden. This oral tradition was put down in writing during the second century AD, but it is difficult to suppose that Jesus himself was unaware of its teaching. Maybe he had intuitional hints of it as a child, and it was among the questions he put to the doctors of the temple when he was twelve.

The devotional sayings and teaching were formally systematized in the sixth century AD, and collectively called 'The Kabbalah.' Many of its concepts resonate closely with words of Jesus himself. Look at some of the following:

- 'You are walking in the presence of God while being right here in this world.'

- 'You become *a dwelling place* of the Divine.'

- 'Prepare to meet your God. Select a special place where no one in the world can hear your voice. Be totally alone. Sit in one spot in the room or in the loft, and do not reveal your secret to anyone. As you prepare…be careful to empty your mind of all mundane vanities. Wrap yourself in your prayer-shawl and put texts on your head so that you will be filled with the awe of the divine Presence who is with you this moment…'

- 'After all, you are physical—flesh and blood. So ultimately holiness is a gift…Be persistent in learning how to sanctify what you do.

The Blessed One will guide you on the path that he wishes, so that you become holy, attaining union continuously. Even your bodily functions are turned into holy deeds. '

- 'We cannot estimate our own inner abundance. Our inner world is linked to a hidden something, a world that is not our world, not yet perceived nor probed. There everything teems with richness; everything sings, celebrates, serves, develops, evolves, uplifts, aspires to be arranged in oneness.'[4]

Today sometimes the ideas within this strand of Jewish mysticism have been usurped and misapplied. This should not dissuade us from realizing that in his time Jesus was very likely to have been familiar with the theory and practice of silent prayer, this deep resting in God. Postures, methods, breathing, and single-minded focusing are all integral to the early Judaic practice of prayer beyond words. In Matt 13.52 Jesus asks, 'Have you understood all these things?' 'Yes,' they answered. So he said to them, 'You will see that a disciple of the kingdom is like a householder who can produce from his store things both new and old.' Jesus seldom preached overtly on meditation, he simply did it, just as he did not preach on making breakfast, he simply did it.

What Stillness is Not

Some misapprehensions of stillness are that it is:

- Being lazy! It has been called 'wasting time *for God.*'
- An abrogation of self-responsibility; it is not about 'I can just chill out and let God do it all.'
- A place to which I can escape—to escape working on difficult personal issues.
- A slot for sleepiness, although indeed sometimes God knows that is what a person most needs. Suggestions to help any tendency to doze off by mistake are made in chapter 4 under 'Distractions.'
- A place I can go to for private comfort and consolation, a soft teddy bear cushion. On the whole, religion does not offer a cosy and absorbent buffer against the world. Mature prayer is about sharpening our hunger, our longing to be with God, and to stand closer to God's will for his world.
- A practice that supersedes attendance at communal worship.
- Primarily about looking at the 'outcomes' for myself. Becoming calmer, sleeping better, and being easier to live with are welcome

incidentals, but they are not the first motive for practising Christian stillness.

- Something that is rather superior to vocal prayer, mine or other's.

What Stillness Is

Stillness means many things, including:

- A letting go of my need to impress—myself or others or God; a letting go of my need to strive and excel; a letting go of my need to constantly justify myself; a letting go of what drives me; a letting go of thinking about myself at all!
- A release, where I can be the self God wants me to be, rather than the self I try to portray or pretend I am, or that others project onto me.
- Getting to a place where God tells and moulds me, rather than me telling God.
- Making a space in time and place where God is the centre and subject, where God is the Presence in which to bask, the Creator in whom to delight.
- A deep remembrance of Jesus' words: 'Let not your heart be troubled, neither let it be afraid...'

William Bridges wrote in 1648 'Oh, you that have refused comfort all this while, receive it in the Lord: walk in the comforts of the Holy Spirit. You that have gone up and down fearing, trembling, doubting, and much discouraged, now at last say..."hope in God, wait on God, trust in God."'

> To wait upon God is to rely and rest upon him.
> According to scriptural phrase, trusting in God is
> the *Recumbency*
> or *Reliance* of the soul upon God;
> it is the *Staying* of the soul,
> It is the *Leaning* of the soul upon the Beloved,
> in *Continual Repose.*'[5]

Stillness is concerned with putting aside all my achievements, excuses, conditioning; it is a place of deep desire, of warm welcome, of coming home. God has said, 'Return to the Rock from which you were hewn.' It is when the tiny fossil that has broken away from its rock-bed returns to its own particular niche, to rest. There I can be swathed by adoration, praise, penitence, concern for others, giving thanks wordlessly, in the awesomeness of the great Presence.

3 Human Energy and the Blueprint of Creation

I am a Bag of Tools for God

Each one us has been created by God to do a specific job for him. Each one of us has been given by the Creator four different areas to our being, and each of these is supplied with tools for the job God is asking us to do. Jesus indicated these four levels when he told us to love the Lord our God with all of our strength (using our bodies, and all the tools packed into that miraculous creation), all of our heart (using the whole palette of emotions), all of our mind (utilizing the great range of rational thinking) and all our soul (aware of the many levels of the spirit).[6] These tools have been lent, not given, and we will have to give an account of how we have used each one. Eventually we return them all to our Maker, as we ourselves return to him.

Sometimes particular tools are taken away from us by circumstances, but on the whole we are responsible for how, when, and where they are used. We need to use them according to the Maker's instructions, and to learn about the properties of the bag that holds them. At times we can lay them aside; either to simply relax, or to offer them back to God for a while so he can cleanse and sharpen them.

Jesus told many parables which highlight this personal responsibility

Jesus told many parables which highlight this personal responsibility. Among them are the wise and foolish bridesmaids, the stewards left with talents, the rich man with his barn, the good Samaritan, the reliable and unreliable servants. It appears to be a major part of his Good News.

Making the Best Use of Our Human Energy

Today, of all the ages since civilization began, experts tell us that we in the industrialized West are subject to the highest levels of stress yet known. We are not subject to the highest level of poverty or disease or exploitation or ignorance. Rather our increased affluence and expectation, mobility, competition and communication have exposed us to an imbalance between demands, and resources and support. In past generations, our levels of energy and the demands made upon it were more or less balanced. The tools with which we were provided and the energy needed to use them seemed to fit together.

Today the endless demands which come at us and the choices which assault us far outweigh the levels of energy available, and our understanding of the equipment we have been lent seems inept and inadequate. More than ever,[7] it is vital that we understand the limits of our energy and the capability of our tools. We have the modelling of Jesus himself to follow, as he deliberately allocated his energy and tools to particular chosen tasks, deciding consciously when to act and when to retract, when to engage and when to disengage, when to expend and when to retreat—and when to pause and simply take in.

This is about understanding the blueprint of God's creation. All animals know of this instinctively. All so-called less developed cultures practise it. It is we of the 'developed' nations who think we can supersede it, and continue gearing ourselves up to ever higher levels of energy expenditure. The records of Jesus' behaviour suggest that he was fully aware of such a principle—a blueprint of creation which goes something like this:

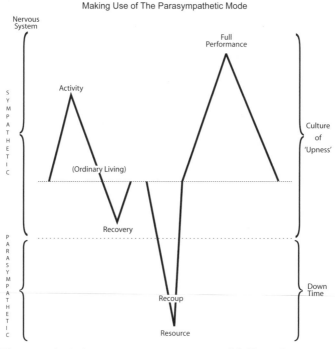

Figure 1 Activity, recovery, resource, and full performance

Whenever we act in a way that is highly stimulated, excitable, and competitive, our energy is sourced from adrenalin and its associated hormones and enzymes, and is delivered via the sympathetic mode of the nervous system. Yet at any time, if we are aware, we can *choose* to switch into the parasympathetic mode.

This equally valid network of nerves—just as much a design of God's invention—enables the levels of our pulse rate, blood pressure, breathing, use of energy and oxygen, all to be lowered. The only function to be raised is our immune efficiency. It is here that we calm down and relax, we can laugh and we can play, the healing process is improved, we can accept paradox and unknowing—and most of all it is here that we can take in from the deep still well of God's love and wisdom. Then we return to active living and find, perhaps to our astonishment, that our full performance is greater than if we had never stopped.

Even Jeremiah moaned, 'This is what Yahweh says about his people "They like to wander here and there, not stopping for a moment, so Yahweh takes no pleasure in them"' (Jer 14.10, CCB).

The practice of deliberately laying down tools has been described by various authorities on prayer in these terms:

- Mechtilde of Magdeburg called it 'sinking and cooling.'

- St John of the Cross described it as 'reaching into the Bare Blind feeling of self.'

- Dame Julian said, 'the Lord wills that we come to him plainly, homely, and nakedly.'

- Meister Eckhart wrote, 'There is nothing so like God as stillness. Love God mindlessly, without mind or mental activities or images or representations. Bare your soul of all mind; and stay there.'

- St Therese of Avila advised that 'God alone rejoices with the soul in deepest silence. There is no reason for the intellect to stir or to seek anything, for the Lord who created it wishes to give it repose.'

At base it is about praying, rather than 'saying our prayers.'

Places Within Stillness

There are myriads of places to be within stillness; many of them carry their own particular school of theory and practice. Just about every one of the world faiths has developed its own level of worship-beyond-words. In the West, the practice of being still in the presence of God has been followed down the ages. Often we cannot find time for 'rest,' and tend to feel that it is something only applicable to those who are weak, or without pressing responsibilities, or those leading lack-lustre lives. But Jesus said, 'Come to me when you are weary and overburdened, and I will give you *rest.*' Jesus would have us restore our souls.

Often we try to make God an object of demands; perhaps we feel safer with a god who needs to be informed and goaded and pleaded with. Then if *we* get it right, God will give us whatever it is we are asking of him. On one occasion a prisoner answered the question 'Why do you come to Chapel?' with an immediate, 'To see what I c'n get out of 'im, i'n it?'

God wants our allegiance, loyalty and love; he already knows our needs

Prisoners come out with more raw honesty than many polite churchgoers, but we are not much different. God wants our allegiance, loyalty and love. He already knows our needs. Perhaps when we still our own energies and concerns in the presence of the creating God two important things can happen. As we are melted before God, he can implant his own signature on us—without us knowing why or how. As we lower all our barriers and defences, God finds a doorway through us into his world.[8]

Objections to Still Prayer

As we observe the unwillingness of most people, including ourselves, to be committed to regular times of stillness, we become aware of objections. Even in the face of our deep need, we find reasons for *not* going into silence, and these continue to baffle our very best intentions. Our ordinary daily living is filled with alternatives which wade into our best plans to give time, energy and selfhood to stillness.

First and foremost there are all the other calls upon our attention which appear to be more worthy and urgent. Jesus somehow never fell into the need to be needed. I, on the other hand, fall into it constantly. So I have to weigh up the importance of any particular task with care and honesty—is this task which clamours so loudly, in fact only a distraction? Is it about what others will think of me? Alternatively, is my true need in fact to take time to receive from God, allowing him to saturate me, before I go out to others? We know that different personality types require different ways of approaching God, and each unique individual's set of priorities has to be honoured. It was St John of the Cross who said 'No two souls travel along the same road to God more than halfway.'[9]

Is my true need in fact to take time to receive from God, allowing him to saturate me, before I go out to others?

Then there is the continual 'I can't find time!' This is a real anxiety, and the last thing God wants is anxiety about meeting him. It is a strange thing that we find time for things we really want to do. If I am hungry, I find time to eat. If I need new clothes, I find time to shop. If I am in love, I find time to meet my lover. Some people like the idea of 'discipline' to make time for stillness; others find it is barely possible to keep to prescribed times, particularly if they have others to care for. It can be a rich gain to practise stillness-in-the-now: whenever there happens to be a pause, or the other is asleep or talking to someone else, or even a personal break in the bathroom. God knows the demands being made upon us and he comes to us, rather than waiting for us to go to him.

God knows the demands being made upon us and he comes to us, rather than waiting for us to go to him

For some, finding time can be a matter of desire and longing, rather than a matter of discipline. One priest who worked with the outcast of the inner city created time out of his 24 hrs by setting his alarm clock for 3am—he got out of bed and celebrated stillness with God before returning to sleep and starting his daily work at 6am. He really wanted to spend time alone with God!

Another difficulty may be of finding space, especially in a lively crowded home. It can help to put into words what you really want to do. A mother of four young children used to say, after returning from work and collecting the family from their various schools, 'You will find I am a nicer mum and we will have a happier tea if you let me have 15 minutes on my own in my room.' They did, and she was a nicer mum, so they knew it was worth it. A quiet corner in a bedroom, a garden seat, the shed, a special place in a church, even the cupboard under the stairs, have all proved useful places to get privacy with God. 'I need space on my own,' said one prisoner to another in his cell, and this enabled the other to take time for himself also, just for a while—another example of personal space, even in the company of others, because it was voiced.

Jung used to say to his secretary, wherever he was, 'There is one unalterable appointment in my diary, every day; it is from 9.00 to 9.30am. It is an appointment with myself.' This formula of 'making an appointment' in my diary is invaluable—I do not have to tell any enquirer what the appointment is about, but simply saying the words 'I have an appointment at that time' carves out the space that is needed.

Distractions in stillness can also be a problem. The 'hows' of dealing with them will be tackled in the next chapter.

'There is one unalterable appointment in my diary, every day; it is an appointment with myself'

Inappropriate Uses of Stillness

Finally in this section, a word about times when an introduction to the practice of stillness is not suitable. There are few of these, but where they occur they are significant.

1 Many people find that immediately following a bereavement or a deep emotional trauma it is unwise to attempt to 'empty' oneself of emotional defences. The associations, memories, remorse that flood in may be too strong, and at this stage are unlikely to encourage rest. Likewise, those who are unwell or depressed may prefer not to take on the demands of concentration which are needed to maintain stillness. Such responses are natural, and usually easy to recognize.

2 Perhaps less easy to recognize are those who live without a firm hold on reality. People who depend on altering consciousness by the use of drugs, or those with schizoid tendencies, should not be urged to attempt stillness. In a professional context, and with a group, some forms of visualization have proved useful, but an enthusiastic encouragement in a church setting may not be helpful.

3 It is inappropriate to attempt to practise stillness when the body is filled with food or alcohol—physiologically it is already over-busy and cannot be relied upon to be still!

To conclude this chapter, I would like to return to Jesus' example of making time and space. The Gospel of John records that after a long and very exhausting day, one that has been full of controversy, 'they all went home.' In the very next verse we read, 'As for Jesus, he went to the Mount of Olives, until daybreak. Then he appeared in the temple again' (John 7.53; 8.1, 2). Here is a moving, living, example of the above 'blueprint of creation.'

4

The Tools Available

God, in his generosity and grace, has equipped us with tools in each area—body, mind, heart and spirit. These are the tools we will need to carry out his will and his work. Traditionally, our churches have downplayed teaching on the use of the body. In some centuries flesh has been seen as a source of evil behaviour, and something to be mastered and overcome. Yet Jesus used images of eating, drinking, washing as the basis of the most sacred acts in our relationship with him—he referred to seeing, hearing, digesting and excreting in his teaching, and used touch, spittle and water as tools of healing.

Every function of the body can be seen as metaphor in prayer. Christianity has been described as the most materialistic of the world faiths. We need to take seriously our responsibility for using the tools of the body, and use them to the glory of God.

It is an amazing fact that the tools which help us get into stillness are the same ones which gear us into activity. The means by which we generate energy in the different levels of our personality are the very ones by which we also strip ourselves of energy, in order to be still and listen. For instance, our joints and muscles can be trained to run a marathon, or they can be trained to lead us into stillness. In the same way the tools of heart, mind and spirit can wind us up, or quieten us down.

Tools of the Body

- As a preparation, many people like to stretch themselves, pulling out the locked-in tension.
- It is good practice to use our senses—to become aware of the sights, sounds, smells around us, and the contact between clothes and skin, chair and limbs.
- Our *musculature* and positioning of the body is of great significance; placing the back, trunk and limbs in such a way that there is no strain or pain, no discomfort or pressure, which could distract from prayer. Jesus himself probably would have followed the Judaic

tradition of praying standing upright. If the feet are apart, each directly under each shoulder, natural gravity helps to keep the position steady. Standing can be held indefinitely, without further effort or concern. Balance is complete; just as Jesus' communion with his Father was complete.

The classic advice is to sit upright in a hard-backed chair, with every cusp of the vertebra resting in the cusp below it. As the spine supports itself it takes a beautiful long 'S' shape, as it was designed to do by its Maker, never in a rigid 'I.'

Some find a meditation stool the ideal way of finding a still position, but if there is a weakness in the back or stiffness in the legs this may be impracticable. Others prefer lying down flat on the floor with a small head-pillow, perhaps with the legs up on a chair so there is no tension between the abdominal muscles and the thighs.

While lying on the floor or the bed, some put their legs straight up the wall at a right angle to their abdomen. In this position the whole circulation of the blood is eased because it returns by gravity, rather than having to be pushed up the legs against gravity as in usual postures. This is an unexpectedly prayerful position. Nevertheless, many teachers say 'Sit back in a familiar chair and be comfortable.'

- On the other hand, some people find meditation comes with mobility. As they focus on walking, running, cycling or even mountaineering, a deep stillness centres them. These activities are outside the scope of the present book.
- The importance of choosing appropriate breathing is expanded in chapter 5.

Whatever position is taken, give thanks for the bodily tools—the muscles and joints, the ligaments and the nerves, the water and the blood and the breath, all the bodily functions and the senses—then deliberately place their energy into the hands of God. Let him take care of it.

Tools of the Mind

Our mental tools include our intellectual energy, the rationality of our learning, the discernment of value, the usefulness of scientific method and our binary thinking as we become familiar with computer skills and modern technology. These are tools to become aware of, to celebrate and for which to give thanks—but then allow to slip away, back into the hands of our Creator.[10] Hanging on to the tools—whatever their value—can be a blockage to the in-coming Holy Spirit who is beyond reason.

Tools of the Heart

The tools of the heart, our emotions and feelings, are immensely powerful. They can swing us into ebullient and joyful states just as strongly as into guilt-ridden, depressed states or into moods of anger, violence, dominance and jealousy. Some people experience considerable fear in going into silence. These are all realities, and are not to be ignored. Emotional energy, whether positive and comforting or even painful and negative, can be used to understand ourselves and others better. In this sense all states of emotion are to be respected; they are all tools of learning. In preparing for stillness it is good simply to be aware of the emotions held at that moment—not the terrors of yesterday or the delights of tomorrow, but what it is I am feeling *now*—and quietly offer that to God to care for. Loosening what clogs me up, clearing the path, so God can move in and sort out the confusions in his way.[11]

Tools of the Spirit

In our spirit the tools lent to us are those of searching and questing, the journeying and yearning, the ache of wanting to return to our origin in the Holy Spirit. As we were born, we brought with us a great homelessness; this is a gap that must be filled, a loss that must be restored, an amputation crying out for healing. We can be re-filled, restored, healed, if and when we get back to God. Only then can I *rest* in the Godhead, as the Godhead has desired. The Holy Spirit himself will pray within; it may appear as wordlessness to me, but the praying of the Spirit is clear to God. He is the knower, I am the known (Romans 8.26). Learning and communal worship is essential but usually done at a different time. In stillness I simply am. I am a human Being, and not a human Doing.

The Choice

The choice of how I use these tools remains with me. When and how I choose to use the tools to either cultivate energy, or allow it to drain away, is my responsibility. If I want to live always stimulated, on the go, at the risk of over-stress—which is the choice of so much of our modern activity—I also have to carry the risks of dis-ease, of brittle relationships, and even breakdown. If I decide sometimes to go into the parasympathetic mode, to explore inner stillness, I will not only reduce those risks but also, which is much more important, put myself in the place of getting closer to the heart of God. There I may grow towards the fullness offered and modelled by Jesus the Christ.

Dealing with Distractions

It is difficult to condense guidance for this real problem into tips, but here are some basics. Anything that is really pressing and consuming can be offered to God for him to deal with, while the one who is praying in stillness receives whatever is necessary to cope with it, later. If the issues continue to press for immediate attention, it can help to jot down names or headings on a piece of paper, so they can be attended to afterwards. If distractions come, just ignore them. Grappling with them, telling them to go away, is giving them attention, just what they want. Deny them that, and the likelihood is that they will fade.

A tendency to doze off by mistake can be met by such techniques as these. Sit relaxed and upright, but with the spine *unsupported*. If a meditation stool is uncomfortable, try sitting on the corner of the bed with feet on the floor each side not under the knees, but as close as possible to the line of the vertical spine. This means that the gravitational centre of the body is along the same plumb line from the ceiling to the floor. Or try keeping the eyelids open, focused on a single small point, like a spot on the wall directly ahead, or a dot on the floor a few feet away.

It is a fact that we process only a few of the sensory stimuli which surround us. To be convinced of this, try stopping still for a moment and become aware of all the sounds, and sights which continue but are not registered. Usually we sift out many of those sounds and sights, and it is totally practicable to develop this natural sifting still further. Purposefully turn off your sensory nerve-endings. Instead of listening *out*, listen *in*; instead of looking *out*, look *in*; instead of reaching *out*wards, reach *in*wards; get *in* touch, receiving *in*sight—the very words we use describe the way. Experience proves that total external quiet is not necessary. Stillness can be real, deep inside us, whatever is going on outside.

Of course it is fine to scratch an itch or clear a throat; no-one will be disturbed. But many find that if physical annoyances such as an itch, a tickly throat, or a rumbling tummy are gently *breathed* into, instead of being attended to directly, they will tend to disappear.

'Chattering monkeys' is the term often given to all those restless and demanding ideas that attack the stillness. We lead such multi-faceted lives, it is hardly surprising that even when we have stilled our bodies and our feelings mental images invade the silence. A physical technique for 'stilling the mind' goes like this:

1   Be conscious of the tension you can lock into a tightly closed fist; now, deliberately loosen the fingers, release the tension and relax. That is something you have done for yourself. The same principle can be applied to the minute muscular tension we use in forming our thoughts.

2   Try to be aware of whether your own thinking is in words or pictures. Some individuals use both. In 'word' thinking, tiny electrical impulses are discharged between the muscles which are used for speech, that is,

verbalization. With 'picture' thinking, similarly minute impulses are exchanged between the muscles we use for seeing, that is, *visualization.*

3   Tense—in a very exaggerated fashion—the muscles of the mouth, cheeks, tongue, soft palate, throat, neck and so on (the muscles used in verbalization). Now discover how to keep those muscles completely still; the words in thinking are eliminated.

4   Equally, if you tense—in a very exaggerated fashion—the muscles that roll the eyeballs up, down, left, right, obliquely up-right, up-left, down-right and down left (the muscles used in visualization), and then consciously keep those very muscles totally still, pictures are eliminated.

5   Result: a quiet mind.

Some say that focusing takes too much effort—it is not relaxing. This objection is based on a misapprehension of what is entailed in focusing. It is not about the fierce concentration needed for a really demanding task, but it means a relaxed single-pointedness of attention. It is bringing to a single point the minimal energy left when the body, heart and mind have been quietened. It is the attention of the spirit being held at one place. Some people use an image to hold this single point; some find that an object such as a cross or a beautiful pebble, perhaps held in the hand, will keep their intention; many find that focusing on their easy breathing is useful. The body will take in new, refreshing oxygen with every gentle breath, and naturally expel the used up, exhausted air, whether we attend to it or not. It is a very accessible way of channelling the soul's energy. Sometimes a prayer word or phrase is attached to each breath, and this is explored in the section entitled *General Selection for Focusing* in the online resources accompanying this booklet on the Grove web site.

When, Where, Who With?

Whenever, wherever, and with whomever, Dame Julian urges us to approach the Godhead 'plainly, homely, nakedly.'[12]

The *When* for any *individual* will have to fit with their personality, their domestic situation, the hours they are expected to work, their health, and a recognition of their own body-clock. There is no 'right' time, morning, afternoon, or evening. It is optimal to choose a time when energy is at its most vital, not when it is sluggish. The focus needed for stripping away barriers to meeting God in stillness requires ego-strength, and not limpid acquiescence. Immediately after a full meal, or following hard exercise, is inappropriate timing. Some replace the classic idea of early morning with a break before lunch (for those out at work, perhaps privacy is found in their parked car) or between coming home and the evening meal. Last thing at night is inadvisable because one is exhausted. Being awake during the night for whatever reason (other than sickness) is quoted in the Psalms as very conducive to stillness (see for example Psalm 4.4; 63.7). Sleep and stillness are physiologically completely different states; but sleep will be improved if it follows a time of stillness.

Any *group* formed to share stillness will have to agree their timing by consensus of all who attend.[13] Sometimes meetings are held before going to work, during the lunchbreak, in the middle evening, or even early on a Saturday morning when the rest of the family are in thrall with the telly. Where the desire is strong enough, the timing will follow. Each group will have its own programme, meeting weekly, fortnightly, monthly or less often. Some groups have a wide base of participants, with the regular attendance of a few.

The *Where* is also variable. Some like churches or church halls, but many people prefer to gather in homes, perhaps rotating between members' houses, or meeting where a member finds they are house-bound. Maybe a shortcut into the place of deep stillness is in a loved picture, or crucifix, book, or handheld object. Music can be helpful, though to some it is distracting. A lit candle can be a great help particularly where concentration begins to fall. Groups have been established not only in homes and churches, but in colleges and airports, hospitals and prisons, marketplaces and gardens, liners and hilltops. The only thing needed is this yearning and longing to listen to God rather than to chatter to God.

The *Who With* is largely a matter of intuition. A deep desire for silence with God is enough to build strong and mutual fellowship. Whether individuals want to talk about 'what went on' during the stillness or not, is a matter for mutual acceptance. To do so can be bonding for some, but if people are going to spend the silence in working out what to say afterwards, it can be negative. The ways of God with each individual soul are so personal and finely tuned and intimate and various, that many people find it inappropriate to verbally 'share' too much. Nonetheless the closeness that develops between people who pray in silence together (whether they 'share' or not) is very powerful.

You may find that children and pets who are allowed to be part of the stillness are adept at it. For children it is like being allowed to return to a deep knowing they were born with, before busy and well-meaning adults interrupted them. Some describe it as 'coming home.' Dogs and cats respond in the same way, although I have yet to still goldfish!

Finally, may I quote Luther? He preceded the 'Simple Way to Pray' with this:

> Dear Master Peter [the friend for whom he wrote the treatise], I will tell you as best I can what I do personally when I pray. May our dear Lord grant to you and to everybody to do it better than I. Amen.

5

Examples for Use

Preparing to Lead a Time of Stillness with a Group

The following initial pointers might be helpful in your preparation:

- The one 'leading' a time of stillness for others should be aware of the vulnerability of those listening, and their dependence on the words offered. In the very practice of letting go they have been 'disarmed.' It is critical for the leader not to use this as an opportunity for evangelization, or of manipulation to his or her own way of thinking.
- The expected length of the quiet should be voiced before it begins, for instance: 'now we'll have a space of 4...12...20 minutes.' The others can then pace themselves and consider the depth to which they are willing to go on that occasion.
- It is important to recognize the interesting difference between this type of silence and that practised by the Quakers. For instance, in a Friends' Meeting the silence can be broken at any moment by a vocal contribution from any member. This means that one has to remain at a level where such a contribution is welcomed. In contrast, when a 'deeper' level is reached, it can be a physiological and damaging shock to be interrupted without warning.
- The practice of stillness needs some layout planning beforehand. This pattern may include any of the following parts: affirmation; recollection; gathering; theme; lead-in and practice; thanksgiving; resolution; inclusion of those not present and concern for others; the Lord's Prayer; and the Grace for each other or doxology—all with the minimum of words. It is not necessary to include each of these inputs in any one session, though that may happen. A great friend said to me 'In prayer, words curb me.'

Now to Begin

We are all, every one of us, beginners; every time we go into stillness we start from scratch. It was Heraclitus, in the fifth century BC, who said, 'We can never step into the same river twice.' *Starting Still Prayer*, below, consists of suggestions for those who may be unused to the idea of stillness as prayer, and would like a full method. Given all the different people finding different paths to God, in the online resources accompanying this booklet two further approaches are offered. The first of these, *Imaging Still Prayer*, is made up of ideas for those who feel more at ease when there is a particular image on which to focus. This imaging prayer is offered with minimal words or description, leaving the imagination free. The imagination is in close contact with the subconscious, and difficult issues there can be dealt with by God directly in this type of prayer. The second, *General Selection for Focusing*, offers a mix-and-match selection for those who want prayer contained in one short phrase. This phrase will 'glow' for them, and then the words may disappear in total absorption before God. The Triune God, Father, Son and Holy Spirit, is attending to each and every soul in the specific way that meets that unique soul.

Adoration, praise and thanksgiving come easily and unselfconsciously in stillness. Penitence and concern for others are integral parts of our relationship with God, but do not necessarily make use of words made familiar to us in communal worship. Andrew Louth has expressed it like this:

> Love is a matter of attention...One can only go out in love from an inwardness that is capable of stillness, of attention, of hearing and perceiving the need of the other...In entering, in stillness, my own heart and coming to know its peculiar waywardness, one enters—not from outside but from within—into the broken condition of all humanity. And in this stillness, the whole of humanity is held close to the healing presence of God. *The Wilderness of God* (DLT, 2003)

Starting Still Prayer: Option 1

All of the following options can be used by an individual on their own or in a group. The words are spoken by the leader:

Affirmation: Glory to God in the highest, peace on earth and goodwill to all creation.

Recollection: The Lord your God is in your midst: the Lord your God will take great delight in you; he will quiet you with his love; he will rejoice over you with singing.' (Trans of Zephaniah 3.17, from Elmore Abbey Speen).

Gathering: We have each come a long way to get here. Behind us we have littered our energy...among people...in places...along the way...Now let us draw our energy gently into this place: this room here, this moment, this now. Energy of body, of mind, of heart, and of soul. Gather those energies into one; focus it all together and give it to God.

Suggestion of theme: Jesus said to his friends 'Come apart, and rest awhile.' Let us follow him, resting with Jesus, and with his disciples.

Lead-in

- To start with, become aware of the remnants of energy that are locked into your joints, your muscles and nerve-endings. Let those knots melt...and fade...and drain away...let the unwanted tension slip away out of your body into whatever it is that is supporting you. You can pick up fresh energy again, later, but for now you do not need it, so let it go...
- Next look at the energy trapped into your mind...all those thoughts running about, those ideas and things you do not want to forget. The useful ones will come back to you later, but for now let them rest, you do not need them at the moment, let them go. Make space in your mind for God to take charge. Make room for God to move.
- Now, take a look at your feelings...perhaps they are rampant, tumultuous, distracting; try to recognize what it is that you are feeling. They may be noisy for your attention...but ask them to lie down for now, for a little while, and you will be attend to them later...The more they can be quiet now, the better they will be served later... Give them back into the hands of God, who gave them to you. He will take care of them for now.
- Lastly, and deepest of all, be aware of the activity in your spirit, the questioning, the searching, the longing...these things are right and proper, but leave them alone for the next little while...let them just slip away back to their source, God. Rest in God.

Practice

Colours of Creation: In the blankness of your mind, let there be a focus on one small spot of brilliant yellow. It is the courageous yellow of the first crocus spear of Spring. The courage of spearing through the hard cold earth...the *courage* in God's creation. Stay with that brilliant yellow spot...

30 second pause

Let the image expand into a small bed of massed red tulips, joyful red. They are the *joy* in God's creation. Stay with that joyful red...

30 second pause

The year moves on and the bed of tulips is replaced by a wide meadow of new green corn, the green of creativity, of newness and growth. A wide meadow of new green corn, focus on the *creativity* of God's creation. Stay with that new green...

30 second pause

And the year moves on. It is summer, and the meadow slopes down to a bay that reaches as far as the eye can see, a bay of the purest blue, stretching out to the horizon. The *purity* of God's creation; stay with that pure blue...

30 second pause

And the year moves on; night falls, and it is tropical night. You find yourself at the centre of a vast hemisphere of the most profound purple; it is the deep purple of the peace of God's creation. You can let yourself be lost in that deep purple peace, it is the peace that passes all understanding. Let it absorb you, and be absorbed by it, the profound peace of God.

Silence for 15–20 mins

Thanksgiving: 'Thanks be to God, who created us…'

Resolution: To do with our awareness, and our choice within it. When shall I next meet God?

Inclusion of those not present, and concern for others: Into this sacred pool of stillness, let us bring in all those we love, and who love us…all those who have asked for our prayer, and those who would ask if they knew how to…all the concerns and causes in the world which lie high on our hearts…asking God to include them under his wings, and embrace them in the way he knows best.

The Lord's Prayer: The leader should always specify whether the traditional or modern version is to be used. Some groups like to stand in a circle and join hands for this.

Blessing/the Grace/Doxology: Together, for each other 'May the grace of our Lord Jesus Christ, the love of God, and the fellowship of the Holy Spirit, be with us all, evermore. Amen.'

Option 2

Affirmation: In the name of God the Father, God the Son, and God the Holy Spirit, the *ruach*, the wind, the inspiriting, the breath, the inspiration that comes from we know not where, and goes where we know not, always in communion with the Godhead.

Recollection: And God breathed into his nostrils the breath of life, and he became a living soul (Gen 2.7 AV).

Gathering: Perhaps, to get here, our breathing grew faster and higher. Now, as we settle down, let us become aware of it: listen to your own breathing for few moments…watch it get slower and lower…

Suggestion of theme: Breathing the breath of God.

Lead-in and practice: Sometimes we forget that we can choose, consciously, between three different types of breathing, each with its own function. First, just imagine you are breathing through two holes in the top of your head: it is the sort of breathing we do when we have a great deal to get through, a great many plans to discharge. It is high up and taut (as you can hear in my voice) and is inappropriate for this moment; so I am going to deliberately bring the centre of my breathing from the top of my head down the back of my neck, into my spine, letting it drop lower and lower, until I know the centre of my breathing lies in the centre of my chest. *Pause.* As I breathe with my chest I can feel the bones of my ribcage heaving up against gravity, and the heavy bones of my shoulders being lifted also against gravity. Chest breathing is very active breathing. I also know that the heart is in the centre of my chest, and the heart is said to be the centre of the emotions. When I am emotional I heave great sighs of breath. So chest breathing is useful for activity and emotion, but is inappropriate for this moment. Gradually I am going to allow the centre of my breathing to slide down the back of my spine...lower and lower, until I am aware that it is in the centre of my body; it has settled in my abdomen. *Pause.*

Each of us has a different rhythm to our breathing, and our own bodies will teach us the most comfortable timing of breaths. The soft, boneless, jointless, wall of the abdomen will slightly swell out and gently fall back...slightly swell out and gently fall back...until I notice that it is the only movement in my entire body. My chest and shoulders are totally still, all my limbs are resting and still. At the centre of my body there is a feeling of warmth and deep ease, and this relaxation is going to spread outwards, like the concentric circles in a pool, slowly and gradually through my entire body. The deep ease spreads into my thighs and trunk, the muscles there becoming long and relaxed...it spreads into my lower legs and shoulders and arms: they are heavy and limp...It spreads further into the hundreds of tiny muscles at the extremity of my body—my hands and fingers, feet and toes, neck and face—all the tiny muscle I usually keep on the alert can go off duty...The whole of me is relaxed, receptive, listening; the only movement of breathing still at the centre, but it is a very slow, soft, low movement.

'And Jesus came into the room and breathed on them...He said 'Receive...' *Pause.* 'Receive ye...' *Pause.* 'Receive ye the Holy Spirit...' (John 20.22 AV). *Stillness for 10, 15, 20 mins*

Thanksgiving: And the breath came into them, and they lived (Ez 37.10 AV).

Resolution: Can I choose to breathe from the centre more often?

Inclusion of those not present: and the Lord's Prayer, as above.

Blessing/the Grace/Doxology: Together: Breathe on us, breath of God, fill us with life anew; that we may love what Thou dost love, and do what Thou wouldst have us do. In Jesus Christ's name, Amen.

Option 3

Affirmation: You are the Rock, O Lord, perfect in all your works. A faithful God, your ways are in truth and unerring uprightness (Deut 32.4).

Recollection: Strong is his dwelling place, and thou puttest thy nest in the rocks (Numbers 24.21). Who is a rock save our God? (Psalm 18.31).

Gathering: The Lord knoweth the thoughts of man, that they are but a puff of smoke. When I say 'My foot slippeth,' Thy mercy, O Lord held me up. The Lord is my strong tower: and my God is the rock of my refuge (Psalm 94).

Suggestion of theme: The power of God's encouragement and support.

Lead-in and practice: Outscape—Inscape
We have been using our eyes to communicate with each other, and that is good. But for the next little while we are going to switch off our outsight in order to gain insight. *Pause.*

We have been using our ears to listen to one another, and that is good. But for the next little while we are going to switch off listening out, in order to listen in. *Pause.*

We have been using words to exchange ideas, and that has been good. But for the next little while we are going to switch from outwards, to inwards. *Pause.*

We have been using our sense of touch to contact each other. But for this next little while we will be getting in touch with God who is within. *Pause.*

I am going to offer a single familiar sentence to focus our thoughts. Try not to think about the words, let them just roll around over and over inside, until they sink lower and lower into your subconscious. To help with this, every few minutes I shall shorten the sentence, until we are left with one syllable; we will stay with that one syllable for 5/10/15 minutes

Be still and know that I am *God*...
Be still and know that I *am*...
Be still and *know*...
Be *still*...
Be...

A space of three or four minutes can be allowed between each statements

Readers will think of other texts that can be used in this way, such as:

Be/hold!/I am/creating/all/things/new
Be/hold!/I am/with you/always

Thanksgiving: Thanks be to God.

Resolution: Personal and private. Or 'Prayer oneth the soul to God.' Dame Julian, *Revelations.*

Inclusion of those not present, and concern for others: and the Lord's Prayer, as above in Option 1.

Blessing/the Grace/Doxology: For each other, let us say together—May the grace of our Lord Jesus Christ, the love of God, and the fellowship of the Holy Spirit, be with us all, evermore. Amen.

As we become more familiar with stillness and waiting, the words we use become fewer and fewer. The deepening awareness of God needs time and space. Resources for this, the real tools of stillness, are expanded and diversified on the Grove web site. As our Creator asks of us—wait on the Lord, be still and rest, and he will give you your heart's delight. God too is waiting.

Notes

1 *Julia News,* Summer 2004, abridged.

2 Dame Julian, *Revelations of Divine Love,* Dom Hudleston OSB (ed) (London: Burns Oates, 1952).

3 These forty instances are detailed in W Nash, *Christ, Stress and Glory* (London: DLT, 1997).

4 Daniel C Matt, *The Essential Kabbalah* (Castle Books, 1997) pp 158, 152, 153, 103/4, compacted.

5 William Bridge, *A Lifting Up for the Downcast* (1648) (London: The Banner of Truth Trust, 1961).

6 By 'levels' I mean levels of accessibility, with each level requiring further persistence and depth of awareness.

7 Personally I would say more than ever *for Christians,* with the high expectations we put upon ourselves.

8 A final note to this section: the stillness being described here is not synonymous with mysticism; this is yet another level of experience. For those who are called to 'apophatic' prayer, that of darkness and waylessness and unknowing, meditation can be the first guided step towards it.

9 See R Innes, *Personality Indicators and the Spiritual Life* (Grove Spirituality booklet, S 57).

10 A particular type of 'Discursive' meditation does make use of rational thinking, but once again, its description is not in the remit of this book.

11 The popularity of Ignatian meditation speaks for itself. There are undoubtedly great insights to be given in this way, but it is different from the way of total stillness.

12 *Revelations of Divine Love*

13 See the Bibliography in the accompanying online resources for help with setting up and maintaining such a group.